Diabetic Breakfast for Seniors

40 Quick and Easy Recipes to Fuel Your Day and Stay Healthy

By

James A. Miller

Copyright © [2023] [JAMES A. MILLER]

All rights reserved. No part of this publication may be reproduced, stored in a retrieval system, or transmitted, in any form or by any means, electronic, mechanical, photocopying, recording, or otherwise, without the prior written permission of the copyright holder.

Table Of Content

Introduction

    Understanding Diabetes in Seniors

    Tips for Preparing Diabetic Breakfasts

Quick and Easy Diabetic Breakfast Recipes

    Scrambled Tofu with Veggies

    Overnight Chia Seed Pudding

    Low-carb Veggie Omelette

    Greek Yogurt Parfait with Berries

    Almond Flour Pancakes

    Avocado and Poached Egg Toast

    Berry and Spinach Smoothie

    Cottage Cheese and Fresh Fruit Bowl

Hearty Breakfast Casseroles

    Spinach and Feta Egg Bake

    Turkey Sausage and Veggie Casserole

    Broccoli and Cheese Quiche

    Zucchini and Mushroom Breakfast Strata

Grab-and-Go Diabetic Breakfasts

    Almond Butter and Banana Sandwich

    Breakfast Burritos with Whole Wheat Tortillas

    Apple Cinnamon Muffins

    Energy-Boosting Trail Mix

- Protein-packed Breakfast Bars
- Mini Vegetable Frittatas
- Yogurt and Berry Parfait in a Jar

International Flavors for Diabetic Breakfasts
- Mexican Huevos Rancheros
- Indian Spiced Scrambled Tofu
- Mediterranean Breakfast Wrap
- Chinese Vegetable Congee

Smoothie Bowls and Breakfast Bowls
- Green Smoothie Bowl with Nuts and Seeds
- Acai Berry Bowl with Coconut Flakes
- Quinoa Breakfast Bowl with Fresh Fruit
- Greek Yogurt Bowl with Granola and Honey

Diabetes-Friendly Baked Goods
- Whole Grain Banana Nut Muffins
- Blueberry Oatmeal Breakfast Cookies
- Cranberry Orange Scones
- Pumpkin Spice Breakfast Loaf

Creative Diabetic Breakfast Ideas for Special Occasions
- Smoked Salmon and Cream Cheese Bagels
- Breakfast Quinoa with Roasted Vegetables
- Stuffed Bell Peppers with Egg and Spinach
- Vegetable and Feta Frittata Cups

Beverages to Complement Diabetic Breakfasts
    Sugar-Free Hot Cocoa
    Iced Green Tea with Lemon
    Cucumber and Mint Infused Water
    Low-carb Strawberry Smoothie

Conclusion

Introduction

As seniors progress through their golden years, maintaining good health becomes paramount to leading a fulfilling and enjoyable life. Among the various health concerns that may arise with age, diabetes stands out as a significant challenge for many individuals. Understanding the intricacies of diabetes and its impact on seniors is crucial in developing effective strategies to manage the condition and promote overall well-being.

Understanding Diabetes in Seniors

Diabetes is a chronic metabolic disorder characterized by high blood glucose levels (hyperglycemia) resulting from either insufficient insulin production or ineffective utilization of insulin by the body. In seniors, the risk of developing diabetes increases due to factors such as age-related changes in metabolism, reduced physical activity, and other health conditions.

About 90% to 95% of all confirmed instances of diabetes in seniors are type 2, making it the most prevalent kind of the disease. Unlike type 1 diabetes, which is usually diagnosed in childhood or adolescence, type 2 diabetes typically develops in adulthood, often in later years.

Importance of a Diabetic-Friendly Breakfast

A well-balanced and diabetic-friendly breakfast is a cornerstone of effective diabetes management for seniors. It sets the tone for the day, providing essential nutrients and helping to regulate blood sugar levels. Here are some key reasons why a diabetic-friendly breakfast is of utmost importance:

1. Blood Sugar Control: A nutritious breakfast can help stabilize blood sugar levels after an overnight fast. It prevents significant fluctuations in glucose levels, reducing the risk of hyperglycemia (high blood sugar) or hypoglycemia (low blood sugar).

2. Energy for the Day: Breakfast provides the necessary energy to kickstart the day and participate in daily activities. Balanced meals can prevent energy slumps and improve overall stamina and well-being.

3. Weight Management: A diabetic-friendly breakfast that includes adequate protein and fiber can promote a feeling of fullness and satiety. This can help seniors manage their weight, as excessive body weight is a risk factor for insulin resistance and type 2 diabetes.

4. Nutrient Intake: A well-planned breakfast ensures that seniors receive essential nutrients, vitamins, and minerals. A varied and nutrient-rich morning meal supports overall health, boosts the immune system, and aids in the body's healing and repair processes.

5. Reducing Cardiovascular Risk: A diabetic-friendly breakfast that emphasizes heart-healthy options, such as whole grains, healthy fats, and low-sodium choices, can help reduce the risk of cardiovascular complications associated with diabetes.

6. Enhancing Mood and Cognitive Function: Breakfast affects cognitive function, memory, and mood. A balanced breakfast can improve mental clarity and focus, contributing to better decision-making and emotional well-being throughout the day.

7. Promoting Regular Eating Patterns: Consistency in eating patterns is essential for diabetes management. Eating a healthy breakfast sets the stage for regular meal times, making it easier to control blood sugar levels and manage insulin.

Tips for Preparing Diabetic Breakfasts

When preparing diabetic-friendly breakfasts for seniors, it's essential to focus on nutrient-dense and low-glycemic options. Here are some practical tips to create delicious and healthful morning meals:

1. Emphasize Whole Foods: Incorporate whole, unprocessed foods into breakfast recipes. Choose whole grains (e.g., oats, quinoa) over refined grains (e.g., white bread) and fresh fruits instead of fruit juices.

2. Include Lean Proteins: Protein helps stabilize blood sugar levels and promotes satiety. Opt for lean protein sources like eggs, Greek yogurt, tofu, lean poultry, and nuts.

3. Add Fiber-Rich Ingredients: Fiber slows down the absorption of sugar and contributes to better blood sugar control. Include vegetables, fruits, nuts, seeds, and whole grains in breakfast recipes.

4. Minimize Added Sugars: Avoid using refined sugars and sugary syrups in recipes. Instead, opt for natural sweeteners like stevia, erythritol, or small amounts of honey or maple syrup if necessary.

5. Watch Portion Sizes: Seniors may have different calorie and nutrient needs. Adjust portion sizes accordingly, considering individual health conditions and activity levels.

6. Control Carbohydrates: Be mindful of carbohydrate content, as it directly impacts blood sugar levels. Distribute carbohydrates evenly throughout the day to avoid spikes.

7. Experiment with Herbs and Spices: Use herbs and spices to add flavor to breakfast dishes without relying on excessive salt, sugar, or unhealthy fats.

Quick and Easy Diabetic Breakfast Recipes

Scrambled Tofu with Veggies

Prep Time: 10 minutes

Cooking Time: 10 minutes

Serve: 2

Ingredients:

- 1 firm tofu block, drained and crumbled
- 1 tablespoon extra-virgin olive oil
- 1/2 cup chopped (any color) bell peppers
- 1/2 cup chopped onions
- 1 cup spinach leaves, baby
- 1 minced garlic clove
- 1 tsp nutritional yeast (optional for cheesy taste)
- 1/2 teaspoon turmeric powder
- Season with salt and pepper to taste.

- Garnish with fresh herbs (such as cilantro or parsley) if desired.

Preparation:
1. Warm the olive oil in a large pan over medium heat.
2. Sauté the diced onions and bell peppers in the pan for 3-4 minutes, or until softened.
3. Cook for another minute after adding the minced garlic.
4. Toss the crumbled tofu in the pan with the turmeric powder, nutritional yeast (if using), salt, and pepper. Cook for 5-6 minutes, or until the tofu is cooked through and gently browned.
5. Cook for another minute, or until the young spinach leaves have wilted.
6. Remove from the heat and, if wanted, garnish with fresh herbs. Serve hot.

Nutritional Value (per serving):

Calories: 180 kcal

Protein: 15g

Carbohydrates: 8g

Fiber: 3g

Fat: 11g

Saturated Fat: 1.5g

Sodium: 220mg

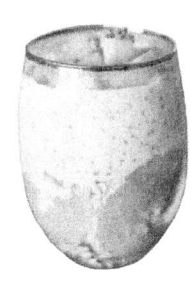

Overnight Chia Seed Pudding

Prep Time: 5 minutes (+ chilling time)

Cooking Time: 0 minutes

Serve: 2

Ingredients:

- 1 tablespoon chia seeds
- 1 cup unsweetened almond milk (or other milk of choice)
- 1 tbsp maple syrup (modify according to taste)
- a half teaspoon of vanilla extract
- Toppings: fresh berries or sliced fruits

Preparation:
1. Combine the chia seeds, almond milk, maple syrup, and vanilla extract in a mixing dish.
2. Stir thoroughly to ensure that the chia seeds are uniformly dispersed.
3. Refrigerate the bowl for at least 4 hours, ideally overnight, to allow the chia seeds to absorb the liquid and form a pudding-like consistency.
4. Give it a thorough swirl before serving. If the pudding is too thick, add a bit more almond milk until the required consistency is reached.
5. Before serving, top with fresh berries or sliced fruits.

Nutritional Value (per serving):

Calories: 150 kcal

Protein: 5g

Carbohydrates: 15g

Fiber: 9g

Fat: 8g

Saturated Fat: 0.5g

Low-carb Veggie Omelette

Prep Time: 10 minutes

Cooking Time: 10 minutes

Serve: 1

Ingredients:

- 3 large eggs
- 1/4 cup diced bell peppers (any color)
- 1/4 cup diced tomatoes
- 1/4 cup chopped spinach or kale
- 1/4 cup sliced mushrooms
- 1/4 cup shredded cheddar cheese (optional)
- 1 teaspoon olive oil
- Salt and pepper to taste
- Fresh herbs (such as parsley or chives) for garnish (optional)

Preparation:

1. Whisk the eggs with a sprinkle of salt and pepper in a mixing bowl until thoroughly mixed.
2. Heat the olive oil in a nonstick skillet over medium heat.

3. Sauté the chopped bell peppers for 2 minutes, or until softened.
4. Cook for another 2 minutes after adding the sliced mushrooms.
5. Sauté the chopped spinach or kale and diced tomatoes for another 1-2 minutes, or until the veggies are soft.
6. Pour the whisked eggs over the skillet's sautéed veggies. Tilt the skillet to ensure that the eggs are distributed evenly.
7. Cook for 3-4 minutes, or until the edges are set. Sprinkle shredded cheddar cheese (if using) over one half of the omelette.
8. Carefully fold the other half of the omelette over the cheese-covered side.
9. Cook for another minute until the cheese melts and the omelette is fully set.
10. Slide the omelette onto a plate, garnish with fresh herbs if desired, and serve hot.

Nutritional Value (per serving):

Calories: 320 kcal

Protein: 23g

Carbohydrates: 8g

Fiber: 2g

Fat: 22g

Saturated Fat: 7g

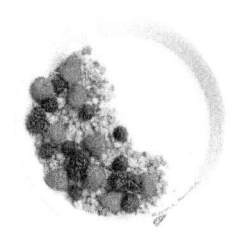

Greek Yogurt Parfait with Berries

Prep Time: 5 minutes

Cooking Time: 0 minutes

Serve: 1

Ingredients:

- 1 cup plain Greek yogurt (unsweetened)
- 1/2 cup berries (strawberries, blueberries, raspberries, etc.)
- 1 tablespoon granola, unsweetened
- 1 teaspoon chopped nuts (almonds or walnuts)
- 1 tsp honey (optional) (for sweetness)
- Garnish with fresh mint leaves (optional).

Preparation:

1. Begin arranging the ingredients in a serving glass or dish. Begin at the bottom with a layer of Greek yogurt.
2. On top of the yogurt, put a layer of mixed berries.
3. Sprinkle a tablespoon of unsweetened granola over the berries.
4. Add a layer of chopped nuts on top of the granola.
5. Drizzle a teaspoon of honey over the nuts if desired for extra sweetness.
6. Repeat the layering process if using a taller glass or bowl.
7. Garnish with fresh mint leaves if desired and serve immediately.

Nutritional Value (per serving):

Calories: 250 kcal

Protein: 15g

Carbohydrates: 25g

Fiber: 5g

Fat: 10g

Saturated Fat: 1.5g

Almond Flour Pancakes

Prep Time: 10 minutes

Cooking Time: 10 minutes

Serve: 2 (makes about 6 pancakes)

Ingredients:

- 1 cup almond flour
- 2 large eggs
- 1/4 cup unsweetened almond milk (or other milk of choice)
- 1 tablespoon melted coconut oil (or butter)
- 1 tablespoon maple syrup (optional, for sweetness)
- 1/2 teaspoon baking powder
- 1/2 teaspoon vanilla extract
- Pinch of salt
- Fresh berries or sliced fruits for topping
- Maple syrup or honey for drizzling (optional)

Preparation:

1. In a mixing bowl, whisk the eggs with almond milk, melted coconut oil (or butter), and maple syrup (if using) until well combined.

2. Add almond flour, baking powder, vanilla extract, and a pinch of salt to the egg mixture. Stir until the pancake batter is smooth.
3. Warm a nonstick pan over medium heat and gently coat with coconut oil or butter.
4. For each pancake, pour roughly 1/4 cup of the pancake batter into the skillet.
5. Cook for 2-3 minutes on each side, or until golden brown and heated through.
6. Remove the pancakes from the griddle and continue the process until the batter is gone.
7. Stack the pancakes on a plate and top with fresh berries or sliced fruits.
8. Drizzle with maple syrup or honey if desired and serve warm.

Nutritional Value (per serving, 3 pancakes):

Calories: 420 kcal

Protein: 16g

Carbohydrates: 14g

Fiber: 5g

Fat: 35g

Saturated Fat: 7g

Avocado and Poached Egg Toast

Prep Time: 5 minutes

Cooking Time: 10 minutes

Serve: 2

Ingredients:

- 2 slices whole-grain bread (low-carb option available if preferred)
- 1 ripe avocado, sliced
- 2 large eggs
- 1 teaspoon white vinegar
- Salt and pepper to taste
- Red pepper flakes or hot sauce for extra spice (optional)
- Garnish with fresh herbs (such as chives or parsley) if desired.

Preparation:

1. Toast the whole-grain bread slices until gently browned and crisp.
2. Fill a small pot halfway with water and add the white vinegar while the bread toasts. Bring the water to a low boil.

3. Each egg should be cracked into a small basin or cup.
4. Using a spoon, create a gently vortex in the boiling water and delicately slip each egg into the middle of the whirlpool. The swirling motion will aid in wrapping the egg whites around the yolk for poaching.
5. Poach the eggs for 3-4 minutes for runny yolks or longer for firmer yolks.
6. Using a slotted spoon, remove the poached eggs from the water and drain any excess water.
7. Spread avocado slices on each toasted bread piece evenly.
8. Top each avocado-covered toast with a poached egg.
9. If desired, season with salt, pepper, red pepper flakes, or spicy sauce.
10. Garnish with fresh herbs and serve immediately.

Nutritional Value (per serving):

Calories: 220 kcal

Protein: 11g

Carbohydrates: 16g

Fiber: 6g

Fat: 14g

Saturated Fat: 3g

Berry and Spinach Smoothie

Prep Time: 5 minutes

Cooking Time: 0 minutes

Serve: 1

Ingredients:

- 1 cup fresh spinach leaves
- 1/2 cup berries (strawberries, blueberries, raspberries, etc.)
- 1/2 banana, ripe
- 1/2 cup unsweetened almond milk (or other milk of choice)
- 1 teaspoon chia seeds
- 1 tsp honey (optional) (for sweetness)
- Ice cubes are optional.

Preparation:

1. Blend together the fresh spinach leaves, mixed berries, ripe banana, almond milk, chia seeds, and honey (if using) in a blender.
2. Blend until the mixture is smooth and creamy. If you like a cooler smoothie, add ice cubes.
3. Fill a glass halfway with the smoothie and serve immediately.

Nutritional Value (per serving):

Calories: 180 kcal

Protein: 5g

Carbohydrates: 30g

Fiber: 8g

Fat: 5g

Saturated Fat: 0.5g

Sodium: 100mg

Cottage Cheese and Fresh Fruit Bowl

Prep Time: 5 minutes

Cooking Time: 0 minutes

Serve: 1

Ingredients:

- 1 cup low-fat cottage cheese
- 1/2 cup mixed fresh fruits (such as berries, kiwi, pineapple, or mango)
- 1 tablespoon chopped nuts (such as almonds or walnuts)
- 1 teaspoon honey (optional, for sweetness)
- Fresh mint leaves for garnish (optional)

Preparation:
1. In a serving bowl, spoon the low-fat cottage cheese.
2. Top the cottage cheese with mixed fresh fruits.
3. Sprinkle the chopped nuts over the fruits.
4. Drizzle with honey if desired for added sweetness.
5. Garnish with fresh mint leaves if desired and serve immediately.

Nutritional Value (per serving):

Calories: 230 kcal

Protein: 18g

Carbohydrates: 20g

Fiber: 3g

Fat: 10g

Saturated Fat: 2g

Please note that the nutritional values provided are approximate and may vary based on the specific ingredients and brands used. Adjustments to serving sizes or ingredients may also affect the nutritional content.

Hearty Breakfast Casseroles

Spinach and Feta Egg Bake

Prep Time: 15 minutes

Cooking Time: 25 minutes

Serve: 4-6

Ingredients:

- 8 large eggs
- 1 cup baby spinach leaves, chopped
- 1/2 cup crumbled feta cheese
- 1/4 cup diced red bell pepper
- 1/4 cup diced red onion
- 1/4 cup milk (any preferred milk)
- 1 tablespoon olive oil
- 1/2 teaspoon dried oregano
- Salt and pepper to taste

Preparation:

1. Preheat the oven to 375°F (190°C). Cooking spray or olive oil should be used to grease a baking dish.
2. In a large mixing bowl, whisk together the eggs, milk, dried oregano, salt, and pepper.

3. Combine the chopped baby spinach, crumbled feta cheese, diced red bell pepper, and diced red onion in a large mixing bowl.
4. Fill the baking dish halfway with the egg mixture.
5. Bake in the preheated oven for about 20-25 minutes or until the egg bake is set and lightly browned on top.
6. Remove from the oven, let it cool slightly, and slice into servings.
7. Serve warm and enjoy!

Nutritional Value (per serving, based on 4 servings):

Calories: 210 kcal

Protein: 14g

Carbohydrates: 3g

Fiber: 1g

Fat: 16g

Saturated Fat: 6g

Turkey Sausage and Veggie Casserole

Prep Time: 20 minutes

Cooking Time: 40 minutes

Serve: 6-8

Ingredients:
- 1 lb (450g) ground turkey sausage
- 1 cup diced bell peppers (any color)
- 1 cup diced zucchini
- 1 cup diced tomatoes
- 1 cup sliced mushrooms
- 8 large eggs
- 1/2 cup milk (any preferred milk)
- 1 cup shredded cheddar cheese (or any preferred cheese)
- 1 tablespoon olive oil
- 1/2 teaspoon dried thyme
- Salt and pepper to taste

Preparation:
1. Preheat the oven to 375°F (190°C). Cooking spray or olive oil should be used to grease a baking dish.
2. Warm the olive oil in a large pan over medium heat.
3. Cook until the ground turkey sausage is browned and cooked thoroughly in the pan. If required, drain any surplus fat.

4. Add the diced bell peppers, zucchini, diced tomatoes, and sliced mushrooms and mix well. Sauté for 3-4 minutes, or until the veggies have softened somewhat.
5. In a separate dish, mix together the eggs, milk, dried thyme, salt, and pepper.
6. In a greased baking dish, evenly distribute the sautéed turkey sausage and vegetable mixture.
7. Over the sausage and veggies, pour the egg mixture.
8. Sprinkle the shredded cheddar cheese on top.
9. Bake in the preheated oven for about 35-40 minutes or until the casserole is set and the cheese is melted and lightly browned.
10. Remove from the oven, let it cool slightly, and slice into servings.
11. Serve warm and enjoy!

Nutritional Value (per serving, based on 6 servings):

Calories: 310 kcal

Protein: 24g

Carbohydrates: 6g

Fiber: 1g

Fat: 21g

Saturated Fat: 8g

Broccoli and Cheese Quiche

Prep Time: 20 minutes

Cooking Time: 40 minutes

Serve: 6

Ingredients:

- 1 store-bought or homemade pie crust
- 2 cups broccoli florets, blanched and chopped
- 1 cup shredded cheddar cheese (or any preferred cheese)
- 4 large eggs
- 1 cup milk (any preferred milk)
- 1/4 cup diced red onion
- 1 tablespoon olive oil
- 1/2 teaspoon dried thyme
- Salt and pepper to taste

Preparation:

1. Preheat the oven to 375°F (190°C).
2. Warm the olive oil in a pan over medium heat.

3. Sauté the chopped red onion for 2 minutes, or until softened.
4. Cook for another 2 minutes after adding the blanched and sliced broccoli florets.
5. In a separate dish, mix together the eggs, milk, dried thyme, salt, and pepper.
6. The pie crust should be used to line a pie plate.
7. Evenly distribute the sautéed broccoli and onion mixture over the pie crust.
8. Top the veggies with the crumbled cheddar cheese.
9. Over the veggies and cheese, pour the egg mixture.
10. Bake for 35-40 minutes, or until the quiche is set and the crust is golden brown, in a preheated oven.
11. Remove from the oven, let it cool slightly, and slice into servings.
12. Serve warm and enjoy!

Nutritional Value (per serving, based on 6 servings):

Calories: 310 kcal

Protein: 15g

Carbohydrates: 15g

Fiber: 2g

Fat: 21g

Saturated Fat: 9g

Zucchini and Mushroom Breakfast Strata

Prep Time: 20 minutes (+ chilling time)

Cooking Time: 45 minutes

Serve: 6-8

Ingredients:

- 6 cups cubed day-old bread (such as whole-grain or white)
- 1 cup diced zucchini
- 1 cup sliced mushrooms
- 1 cup shredded cheddar cheese (or any preferred cheese)
- 8 large eggs
- 1 1/2 cups milk (any preferred milk)
- 2 tablespoons olive oil
- 1 tablespoon Dijon mustard
- 1 teaspoon dried thyme
- Salt and pepper to taste

Preparation:
1. Warm the olive oil in a large pan over medium heat.
2. Sauté the diced zucchini and sliced mushrooms in the pan for 3-4 minutes, or until slightly softened.
3. In a large mixing bowl, whisk together the eggs, milk, Dijon mustard, dried thyme, salt, and pepper.
4. Cooking spray or olive oil should be used to grease a baking dish.
5. In a greased baking dish, equally distribute half of the cubed bread.
6. On top of the toast, layer half of the sautéed zucchini and mushrooms.
7. Half of the shredded cheddar cheese should be sprinkled over the veggies.
8. Repeat the layering process with the remaining bread, zucchini, mushrooms, and cheese.
9. Pour the egg mixture evenly over the layers in the baking dish, ensuring that all the bread is soaked in the egg mixture.

10. Cover the baking dish with plastic wrap and refrigerate for at least 2 hours or preferably overnight to allow the bread to absorb the egg mixture.
11. Preheat the oven to 375°F (190°C).
12. Remove the baking dish from the refrigerator and set it aside for about 10 minutes to come to room temperature.
13. Bake the strata in the preheated oven for about 40-45 minutes or until it is set in the center and the top is golden brown.
14. Remove from the oven and let it cool for a few minutes before slicing into servings.
15. Serve warm and enjoy this delicious and savory breakfast strata.

Nutritional Value (per serving, based on 6 servings):

Calories: 310 kcal

Protein: 15g

Carbohydrates: 25g

Fiber: 2g

Fat: 16g

Saturated Fat: 6g

Grab-and-Go Diabetic Breakfasts

Almond Butter and Banana Sandwich

Prep Time: 5 minutes

Cooking Time: 0 minutes

Serve: 1

Ingredients:

- 2 slices whole-grain bread
- 2 tablespoons almond butter
- 1 ripe banana, sliced
- 1 teaspoon honey (optional, for sweetness)
- Cinnamon powder (optional, for extra flavor)

Preparation:

1. Lay out the slices of whole-grain bread.
2. Spread almond butter on one side of each bread piece equally.
3. Place one slice of bread on top of the cut bananas.
4. If desired, drizzle honey over the bananas and sprinkle with cinnamon powder for added taste.
5. To make a sandwich, place the second bread piece, almond butter side down, on top.
6. Gently press the sandwich together.

7. Leave the sandwich intact or cut it in half.
8. Serve immediately or wrap it up for a quick on-the-go breakfast.

Nutritional Value (per serving):

Calories: 380 kcal

Protein: 10g

Carbohydrates: 56g

Fiber: 10g

Fat: 16g

Saturated Fat: 1.5g

Breakfast Burritos with Whole Wheat Tortillas

Prep Time: 15 minutes

Cooking Time: 10 minutes

Serve: 4

Ingredients:

- 4 large whole wheat tortillas
- 6 large eggs
- 1 cup black beans, cooked and drained
- 1/2 cup diced bell peppers (any color)
- 1/2 cup diced onions

- 1/2 cup shredded cheddar cheese
- 1 tablespoon olive oil
- 1 teaspoon chili powder
- Salt and pepper to taste
- Salsa or hot sauce for serving (optional)

Preparation:

1. Warm the olive oil in a large pan over medium heat.
2. Sauté the diced onions and bell peppers in the pan for 3-4 minutes, or until softened.
3. In a mixing dish, add the eggs, chili powder, salt, and pepper.
4. Pour the whisked eggs over the sautéed veggies in the skillet.
5. Scramble the eggs with the vegetables until they are fully cooked.
6. Warm the whole wheat tortillas in a separate skillet or microwave to make them pliable.
7. Lay out the tortillas and divide the scrambled eggs, black beans, and shredded cheddar cheese among them.

8. Fold the sides of the tortillas over the fillings and then fold the bottom up over the sides to form a burrito.
9. Roll up the burritos tightly.
10. Serve immediately or wrap them in foil for a portable breakfast.

Nutritional Value (per serving):

Calories: 370 kcal

Protein: 18g

Carbohydrates: 32g

Fiber: 8g

Fat: 19g

Saturated Fat: 6g

Apple Cinnamon Muffins (Sugar-Free)

Prep Time: 15 minutes

Cooking Time: 20 minutes

Serve: 12 muffins

Ingredients:

- 2 cups whole wheat flour
- 2 large apples, grated
- 1/2 cup unsweetened applesauce

- 1/4 cup olive oil
- 1/4 cup unsweetened almond milk (or other milk of choice)
- two huge eggs
- 1 tbsp. baking powder
- 1 teaspoon cinnamon powder
- a half teaspoon of vanilla extract
- 1 teaspoon salt

Preparation:

1. Preheat the oven to 375 degrees Fahrenheit (190 degrees Celsius). Line a muffin tray with paper liners or grease it.
2. In a large mixing bowl, combine the whole wheat flour, baking powder, ground cinnamon, and salt.
3. In a separate bowl, whisk the eggs with olive oil, unsweetened applesauce, unsweetened almond milk, and vanilla extract until well combined.
4. Mix the wet and dry ingredients together until barely mixed.
5. Incorporate the grated apples into the batter.

6. Fill each muffin cup 3/4 full with batter from the prepared muffin tray.
7. Bake for 18-20 minutes in a preheated oven, or until a toothpick inserted into the middle of a muffin comes out clean.
8. Remove from the oven and rest for a few minutes in the pan before transferring to a wire rack to cool entirely.
9. Serve the muffins as a delicious and healthy sugar-free breakfast treat.

Nutritional Value (per muffin):

Calories: 150 kcal

Protein: 3g

Carbohydrates: 20g

Fiber: 3g

Fat: 6g

Saturated Fat: 1g

Energy-Boosting Trail Mix

Prep Time: 5 minutes

Cooking Time: 0 minutes

Serve: About 8 servings

Ingredients:

- 1 cup raw almonds
- 1 cup raw cashews
- 1 cup dried cranberries
- 1/2 cup pumpkin seeds
- 1/2 cup unsweetened coconut flakes
- 1/2 cup dark chocolate chips (optional, for added sweetness)

Preparation:

1. In a large mixing bowl, combine all the ingredients: raw almonds, raw cashews, dried cranberries, pumpkin seeds, unsweetened coconut flakes, and dark chocolate chips (if using).
2. Toss the ingredients together until well mixed.
3. Place the trail mix in an airtight container to keep it fresh.
4. As a fast and filling snack, or as a topping for yogurt or porridge.

Nutritional value per serving (8 servings):

Calories: 290 kcal

Protein: 7g

Carbohydrates: 20g

Fiber: 4g

Fat: 21g

Saturated Fat: 7g

Sodium: 10mg

Protein-packed Breakfast Bars

Prep Time: 15 minutes

Cooking Time: 25 minutes

Chilling Time: 1 hour

Serve: 10 bars

Ingredients:

- 1 1/2 cups old-fashioned rolled oats
- 1 cup almond butter (or any nut butter of choice)
- 1/2 cup unsweetened applesauce
- 1/4 cup honey (or any preferred liquid sweetener)
- 1/4 cup protein powder (any flavor)
- 1/4 cup unsweetened shredded coconut
- 1/4 cup chopped nuts (such as almonds or walnuts)
- 1/4 cup dried fruits (such as cranberries or raisins)
- a tsp vanilla extract

- 1 teaspoon salt

Preparation:
1. Use parchment paper to line a baking dish or pan.
2. Combine the almond butter, unsweetened applesauce, honey, and vanilla extract in a large mixing bowl.
3. Mix until smooth and fully mixed.
4. Combine the rolled oats, protein powder, unsweetened shredded coconut, chopped almonds, dried fruits, and a touch of salt in a mixing bowl.
5. Stir everything up until everything is equally combined.
6. Transfer the mixture to the prepared baking dish and smooth it out evenly with the back of a spoon or your fingertips.
7. Refrigerate the baking dish for at least 1 hour to allow the mixture to firm.
8. Once chilled and firm, remove the mixture from the refrigerator and cut it into bars.
9. Store the protein-packed breakfast bars in an airtight container in the refrigerator.

10. Grab a bar whenever you need a convenient and protein-rich breakfast on-the-go.

Nutritional Value (per bar, based on 10 bars):

Calories: 290 kcal

Protein: 10g

Carbohydrates: 22g

Fiber: 4g

Fat: 19g

Saturated Fat: 3g

Mini Vegetable Frittatas

Prep Time: 15 minutes

Cooking Time: 20 minutes

Serve: 6 mini frittatas

Ingredients:

- 6 large eggs
- 1/4 cup milk (any preferred milk)
- 1/2 cup chopped spinach
- 1/4 cup diced bell peppers (any color)
- 1/4 cup diced tomatoes
- 1/4 cup diced onions

- 1/4 cup shredded cheddar cheese (or any preferred cheese)
- 1 tablespoon olive oil
- 1/2 teaspoon dried oregano
- Salt and pepper to taste

Preparation:

1. Preheat the oven to 375°F (190°C). Grease or line a muffin pan with paper liners.
2. In a large mixing bowl, whisk together the eggs, milk, dried oregano, salt, and pepper.
3. Warm the olive oil in a pan over medium heat.
4. Sauté the diced onions for 2 minutes, or until softened.
5. Cook for another 2 minutes after adding the diced bell peppers and diced tomatoes.
6. Cook until the spinach has wilted in the skillet.
7. Remove the skillet from the heat.
8. Divide the sautéed vegetables among the muffin cups in the prepared muffin tin.
9. Pour the egg mixture evenly over the vegetables in each muffin cup.

10. Sprinkle the shredded cheddar cheese over the egg mixture in each cup.
11. Bake in the preheated oven for about 15-20 minutes or until the frittatas are set and lightly browned on top.
12. Remove from the oven and let the mini frittatas cool slightly before removing them from the muffin tin.
13. Serve warm or let them cool completely and store them in the refrigerator for a quick and nutritious breakfast option.

Nutritional Value (per mini frittata, based on 6 servings):

Calories: 110 kcal

Protein: 7g

Carbohydrates: 3g

Fiber: 1g

Fat: 8g

Saturated Fat: 3g

Yogurt and Berry Parfait in a Jar

Prep Time: 10 minutes

Cooking Time: 0 minutes

Serve: 1

Ingredients:

- 1 cup Greek yogurt (or any preferred yogurt)
- 1/2 cup mixed fresh berries (such as strawberries, blueberries, raspberries)
- 2 tablespoons granola (or any preferred crunchy topping)
- 1 tablespoon honey (optional, for sweetness)

Preparation:

1. In a clean jar or glass, layer the Greek yogurt with the mixed fresh berries and granola.
2. Drizzle honey over the layers if desired, for added sweetness.
3. Continue layering until you reach the top of the jar or your desired portion size.
4. Refrigerate the container until ready to serve.

5. When you're ready to eat, simply grab a spoon and enjoy the delicious and wholesome yogurt and berry parfait.

Nutritional Value (per serving):

Calories: 290 kcal

Protein: 18g

Carbohydrates: 32g

Fiber: 4g

Fat: 10g

Saturated Fat: 2g

International Flavors for Diabetic Breakfasts

Mexican Huevos Rancheros

Prep Time: 10 minutes

Cooking Time: 15 minutes

Serve: 2

Ingredients:

- 4 large eggs
- 1 cup washed and drained canned black beans
- 1 cup diced tomatoes
- 1/2 cup diced onions
- 1/2 cup diced bell peppers (any color)
- 1/4 cup chopped cilantro
- 2 tablespoons olive oil
- 2 cloves garlic, minced
- 1 teaspoon ground cumin
- 1 teaspoon chili powder
- Salt and pepper to taste
- 4 small corn tortillas
- 1/4 cup shredded cheddar cheese (or any preferred cheese)

- Salsa and avocado slices for serving (optional)

Preparation:
1. Warm the olive oil in a large pan over medium heat.
2. Add the minced garlic and diced onions to the skillet and sauté until the onions are translucent.
3. Stir in the diced bell peppers, canned black beans, diced tomatoes, ground cumin, chili powder, salt, and pepper.
4. Cook the mixture for about 5-7 minutes until the vegetables are tender and the flavors are well combined.
5. In a separate skillet, fry the corn tortillas until they are lightly browned and crispy on both sides.
6. While the tortillas are frying, prepare the eggs sunny-side up in the same skillet or in a different one.
7. Place a fried tortilla on each platter to serve..
8. Top each tortilla with a portion of the black bean and vegetable mixture.
9. Carefully place a sunny-side-up egg on top of each tortilla.

10. Sprinkle shredded cheddar cheese and chopped cilantro over the eggs.
11. Serve with salsa and avocado slices on the side, if desired.

Nutritional Value (per serving, based on 2 servings):

Calories: 460 kcal

Protein: 22g

Carbohydrates: 44g

Fiber: 12g

Fat: 22g

Saturated Fat: 7g

Indian Spiced Scrambled Tofu

Prep Time: 10 minutes

Cooking Time: 15 minutes

Serve: 2

Ingredients:

- 14 oz (400g) firm tofu, drained and crumbled
- 1/2 cup diced onions
- 1/2 cup diced tomatoes
- 1/4 cup chopped cilantro

- 2 tablespoons olive oil
- 1 teaspoon ground cumin
- 1/2 teaspoon ground turmeric
- 1/2 teaspoon ground coriander
- 1/4 teaspoon cayenne pepper (optional, for heat)
- Salt and pepper to taste
- Toasted whole wheat bread or naan for serving

Preparation:

1. Warm the olive oil in a large pan over medium heat.
2. Sauté the chopped onions in the pan until they are transparent.
3. Stir in the crumbled tofu, ground cumin, ground turmeric, ground coriander, cayenne pepper (if using), salt, and pepper.
4. Cook the tofu mixture for about 5-7 minutes until the spices are well incorporated and the tofu is heated through.
5. Add the diced tomatoes and chopped cilantro to the skillet, and cook for another 2-3 minutes.
6. Taste and adjust seasoning if needed.

7. Serve the Indian spiced scrambled tofu with toasted whole wheat bread or naan for a flavorful and protein-rich breakfast.

Nutritional Value (per serving, based on 2 servings):

Calories: 320 kcal

Protein: 20g

Carbohydrates: 11g

Fiber: 3g

Fat: 22g

Saturated Fat: 3g

Mediterranean Breakfast Wrap

Prep Time: 10 minutes

Cooking Time: 0 minutes

Serve: 2 wraps

Ingredients:

- 2 large whole wheat tortillas
- 1/2 cup hummus (store-bought or homemade)
- 1/2 cup diced cucumbers
- 1/2 cup diced tomatoes
- 1/4 cup chopped Kalamata olives

- 1/4 cup crumbled feta cheese
- 2 tablespoons chopped fresh parsley
- Salt and pepper to taste

Preparation:
1. Lay out the whole wheat tortillas on a clean surface.
2. Spread hummus evenly on each tortilla, leaving a small border around the edges.
3. Place the diced cucumbers, diced tomatoes, chopped Kalamata olives, crumbled feta cheese, and chopped fresh parsley in the center of each tortilla, on top of the hummus.
4. Sprinkle with salt and pepper to taste.
5. Fold the sides of the tortillas over the fillings and then fold the bottom up over the sides to form a wrap.
6. Roll up the wraps tightly.
7. Slice each wrap in half if desired, and serve immediately for a Mediterranean-inspired breakfast delight.

Nutritional Value (per wrap, based on 2 wraps):
Calories: 380 kcal

Protein: 12g

Carbohydrates: 33g

Fiber: 8g

Fat: 22g

Saturated Fat: 6g

Chinese Vegetable Congee

Prep Time: 10 minutes

Cooking Time: 40 minutes

Serve: 4

Ingredients:

- 1 cup white rice (long-grain or jasmine rice)
- 6 cups vegetable broth or water
- 1 cup mixed vegetables (such as carrots, peas, corn)
- 1 cup chopped bok choy or spinach
- 2 cloves garlic, minced
- 1 tablespoon grated ginger
- 2 tablespoons soy sauce (or tamari for gluten-free option)
- 1 tablespoon sesame oil

- 1 tablespoon vegetable oil
- 1 teaspoon white pepper
- Salt to taste
- Sliced green onions and toasted sesame seeds for garnish

Preparation:

1. Rinse the white rice in cold water until it is clear.
2. In a large pot, heat the vegetable oil over medium heat.
3. Add the minced garlic and grated ginger to the pot and sauté for about 1 minute until fragrant.
4. Add the rinsed white rice to the pot and stir to coat the rice with the garlic and ginger.
5. Bring to a boil with the veggie broth or water.
6. Once boiling, reduce the heat to low, cover the pot, and let the rice simmer for about 30-35 minutes until it becomes creamy and fully cooked, stirring occasionally to prevent sticking to the bottom of the pot.
7. Add the mixed vegetables and chopped bok choy or spinach to the pot, and stir to combine.

8. Continue simmering for another 5-7 minutes until the vegetables are tender.
9. Combine the soy sauce (or tamari) and sesame oil in a mixing bowl. Season with salt and white pepper to taste.
10. Turn off the heat in the saucepan.
11. To add flavor and texture, serve the Chinese vegetable congee in bowls topped with sliced green onions and toasted sesame seeds.

Nutritional Value (per serving, based on four):

Calories: 280 kcal

Protein: 5g

Carbohydrates: 46g

Fiber: 3g

Fat: 8g

Saturated Fat: 1g

Smoothie Bowls and Breakfast Bowls

Green Smoothie Bowl with Nuts and Seeds

Prep Time: 10 minutes

Cooking Time: 0 minutes

Serve: 1

Ingredients:

- 1 ripe banana, frozen
- 1 cup fresh spinach leaves
- 1/2 cup frozen pineapple chunks
- 1/2 cup frozen mango chunks
- 1/2 cup unsweetened almond milk (or other milk of choice)
- 1 tablespoon chia seeds
- 1 tablespoon flaxseeds
- 1 tablespoon almond butter
- Toppings: Sliced kiwi, sliced strawberries, sliced almonds, pumpkin seeds, coconut flakes

Preparation:
1. In a blender, combine the frozen banana, fresh spinach leaves, frozen pineapple chunks, frozen mango chunks, almond milk, chia seeds, flaxseeds, and almond butter.
2. Blend until smooth and creamy, adding additional almond milk as required.
3. Pour the green smoothie into a bowl.
4. Top the smoothie with sliced kiwi, sliced strawberries, sliced almonds, pumpkin seeds, and coconut flakes for added texture and flavor.
5. Serve the green smoothie bowl immediately and enjoy a refreshing and nutrient-packed breakfast.

Nutritional Value (per serving):

Calories: 400 kcal

Protein: 10g

Carbohydrates: 57g

Fiber: 12g

Fat: 19g

Saturated Fat: 2g

Acai Berry Bowl with Coconut Flakes

Prep Time: 10 minutes

Cooking Time: 0 minutes

Serve: 1

Ingredients:

- 1 packet frozen acai puree (unsweetened)
- 1 ripe banana, frozen
- 1/2 cup frozen mixed berries (such as blueberries, raspberries, strawberries)
- 1/2 cup unsweetened almond milk (or other milk of choice)
- 1 tablespoon honey (optional, for sweetness)
- Toppings: Sliced bananas, fresh berries, coconut flakes, chia seeds, granola

Preparation:

1. In a blender, combine the frozen acai puree, frozen banana, frozen mixed berries, almond milk, and honey (if using).
2. Blend until smooth and thick, adding more almond milk if needed to help with blending.
3. Fill a bowl halfway with the acai berry mixture.

4. Top the bowl with sliced bananas, fresh berries, coconut flakes, chia seeds, and granola for added texture and flavor.
  5. Serve the acai berry bowl immediately and indulge in a delicious and antioxidant-rich breakfast.

Nutritional Value (per serving):

Calories: 380 kcal

Protein: 5g

Carbohydrates: 60g

Fiber: 11g

Fat: 14g

Saturated Fat: 2g

Quinoa Breakfast Bowl with Fresh Fruit

Prep Time: 15 minutes

Cooking Time: 15 minutes

Serve: 2

Ingredients:

- 1/2 cup quinoa, rinsed
- 1 cup water

- 1 cup diced mixed fresh fruit (such as strawberries, blueberries, mangoes, kiwi)
- 1/4 cup plain Greek yogurt
- 2 tablespoons honey (or any preferred sweetener)
- 1 tablespoon chopped nuts (such as almonds or walnuts)
- 1 tablespoon unsweetened shredded coconut

Preparation:

1. Bring the water to a boil in a small saucepan.
2. Add the rinsed quinoa to the boiling water, reduce the heat to low, cover the saucepan, and let the quinoa simmer for about 12-15 minutes or until all the water is absorbed and the quinoa is fluffy.
3. Remove the saucepan from the heat and let the quinoa cool slightly.
4. In a bowl, mix the cooked quinoa with the diced mixed fresh fruit.
5. Top the quinoa and fruit mixture with a dollop of plain Greek yogurt.
6. Drizzle honey over the bowl for added sweetness.

7. Sprinkle chopped nuts and unsweetened shredded coconut over the top for added crunch and flavor.
8. Serve the quinoa breakfast bowl immediately and enjoy a protein-rich and nutritious morning meal.

Nutritional Value (per serving, based on 2 servings):

Calories: 330 kcal

Protein: 10g

Carbohydrates: 59g

Fiber: 7g

Fat: 8g

Saturated Fat: 2g

Greek Yogurt Bowl with Granola and Honey

Prep Time: 5 minutes

Cooking Time: 0 minutes

Serve: 1

Ingredients:

- 1 cup plain Greek yogurt
- 1/4 cup granola (store-bought or homemade)
- 1/4 cup mixed fresh berries (such as blueberries, strawberries, raspberries)
- 1 tablespoon honey (or any preferred sweetener)

- 1 tablespoon sliced almonds
- 1 tablespoon pumpkin seeds

Preparation:

1. In a bowl, layer the plain Greek yogurt with granola and mixed fresh berries.
2. Drizzle honey over the top for added sweetness.
3. Sprinkle sliced almonds and pumpkin seeds over the bowl for added texture and nutrients.
4. Serve the Greek yogurt bowl immediately and savor the creamy, crunchy, and satisfying breakfast.

Nutritional Value (per serving):

Calories: 380 kcal

Protein: 23g

Carbohydrates: 46g

Fiber: 5g

Fat: 14g

Saturated Fat: 3g

Diabetes-Friendly Baked Goods

Whole Grain Banana Nut Muffins

Prep Time: 15 minutes

Cooking Time: 20 minutes

Serve: 12 muffins

Ingredients:

- 2 cups whole wheat flour
- 1 teaspoon baking soda
- 1/2 teaspoon baking powder
- 1/4 teaspoon salt
- 1/2 teaspoon ground cinnamon
- 1/4 cup unsweetened applesauce
- 1/4 cup olive oil
- 1/2 cup honey (or any preferred sweetener)
- 2 large ripe bananas, mashed
- 2 large eggs
- 1 teaspoon vanilla extract
- 1/2 cup chopped walnuts (or any preferred nuts)

Preparation:
1. Preheat the oven to 375°F (190°C). Line a muffin tray with paper liners or grease it.
2. Whisk together the whole wheat flour, baking soda, baking powder, salt, and powdered cinnamon in a large mixing basin.
3. In a separate dish, whisk together the unsweetened applesauce, olive oil, honey, mashed bananas, eggs, and vanilla extract.
4. Mix the wet and dry ingredients together until barely mixed.
5. Incorporate the walnuts into the muffin batter.
6. Spoon the batter into the prepared muffin tin, filling each cup about 3/4 full.
7. Bake in the preheated oven for about 18-20 minutes or until a toothpick inserted into the center of a muffin comes out clean.
8. Remove from the oven and rest for a few minutes in the pan before transferring to a wire rack to cool entirely.
9. Serve the whole grain banana nut muffins as a delicious and wholesome breakfast treat.

Nutritional Value (per muffin):

Calories: 180 kcal

Protein: 4g

Carbohydrates: 27g

Fiber: 3g

Fat: 7g

Saturated Fat: 1g

Blueberry Oatmeal Breakfast Cookies

Prep Time: 15 minutes

Cooking Time: 15 minutes

Serve: 12 cookies

Ingredients:

- 1 1/2 cups rolled oats
- 1 cup whole wheat flour
- 1 teaspoon baking powder
- 1/4 teaspoon salt
- 1/2 teaspoon ground cinnamon
- 1/4 cup unsweetened applesauce
- 1/4 cup olive oil
- 1/2 cup honey (or any preferred sweetener)

- 1 large egg
- 1 teaspoon vanilla extract
- 1 cup fresh or frozen blueberries

Preparation:

1. Preheat the oven to 350°F (175°C). Using parchment paper, line a baking sheet.
2. In a large mixing bowl, stir together the rolled oats, whole wheat flour, baking powder, salt, and ground cinnamon.
3. In a separate bowl, mix the unsweetened applesauce, olive oil, honey, egg, and vanilla extract until well combined.
4. Mix the wet and dry ingredients together until barely mixed.
5. Fold the blueberries into the cookie batter gently.
6. Drop spoonfuls of cookie dough onto the prepared baking sheet, leaving room for spreading.
7. Use the back of a spoon or your fingertips to softly flatten each cookie.
8. Bake for 12-15 minutes, or until the edges of the cookies are gently brown in a preheated oven.

9. Remove from the oven and rest for a few minutes on the baking sheet before transferring to a wire rack to cool fully.
10. completely.
11. Serve the blueberry oatmeal breakfast cookies as a tasty and portable morning treat.

Nutritional Value (per cookie):

Calories: 170 kcal

Protein: 3g

Carbohydrates: 26g

Fiber: 2g

Fat: 7g

Saturated Fat: 1g

Cranberry Orange Scones (Low Sugar)

Prep Time: 20 minutes

Cooking Time: 20 minutes

Serve: 8 scones

Ingredients:

- 2 cups whole wheat flour
- 1/4 cup granulated sugar (or any preferred sweetener)

- 1 tablespoon baking powder
- 1/4 teaspoon salt
- Zest of 1 orange
- 1/4 cup cold unsalted butter, cubed
- 1/2 cup dried cranberries
- 1/2 cup plain Greek yogurt
- 1/4 cup fresh orange juice
- 1 teaspoon vanilla extract
- 1 large egg, beaten (for egg wash)

Preparation:

1. Preheat the oven to 375°F (190°C). Using parchment paper, line a baking sheet.
2. Whisk together the whole wheat flour, granulated sugar, baking powder, salt, and orange zest in a large mixing basin.
3. Cut the cold unsalted butter into the dry ingredients with a pastry cutter or two forks until the mixture resembles coarse crumbs.
4. Add the dried cranberries and mix well.

5. In a separate dish, thoroughly combine the plain Greek yogurt, fresh orange juice, and vanilla essence.
6. combined.
7. Stir in the yogurt mixture and dry ingredients until a dough forms.
8. Turn out the dough onto a floured surface and knead it lightly a few times until it comes together.
9. Form the dough into a 1-inch-thick round.
10. Make 8 equal wedges out of the dough.
11. Place the scones on the prepared baking sheet, spacing them apart.
12. For a golden finish, brush the tops of the scones with the beaten egg.
13. Bake in the preheated oven for about 18-20 minutes or until the scones are lightly golden on the outside and fully cooked on the inside.
14. Remove from the oven and let the scones cool on the baking sheet for a few minutes before transferring them to a wire rack to cool completely.

15. Serve the cranberry orange scones as a delightful and slightly sweet breakfast option.

Nutritional Value (per scone):

Calories: 270 kcal

Protein: 6g

Carbohydrates: 39g

Fiber: 4g

Fat: 10g

Saturated Fat: 6g

Pumpkin Spice Breakfast Loaf

Prep Time: 15 minutes

Cooking Time: 55 minutes

Serve: 10 slices

Ingredients:

- 1 3/4 cups whole wheat flour
- 1 teaspoon baking soda
- 1/2 teaspoon baking powder
- 1/4 teaspoon salt
- 1 1/2 teaspoons ground cinnamon
- 1/2 teaspoon ground nutmeg

- 1/4 teaspoon ground cloves
- 1 cup canned pumpkin puree
- 1/2 cup honey (or any preferred sweetener)
- 1/4 cup unsweetened applesauce
- 1/4 cup olive oil
- 2 large eggs
- 1 teaspoon vanilla extract
- 1/2 cup chopped pecans or walnuts (optional)

Preparation Method:

1. Preheat the oven to 350°F (175°C). Line a loaf pan with parchment paper or grease it.
2. Whisk together the whole wheat flour, baking soda, baking powder, salt, ground cinnamon, ground nutmeg, and ground cloves in a large mixing basin.
3. In a separate dish, whisk together the canned pumpkin puree, honey, unsweetened applesauce, olive oil, eggs, and vanilla extract.
4. Mix the wet and dry ingredients together until barely mixed.

5. Fold in the chopped pecans or walnuts, if using, into the batter.
6. Pour the batter into the prepared loaf pan and evenly distribute it.
7. Bake for 50-55 minutes in a preheated oven, or until a toothpick inserted into the middle of the loaf comes out clean.
8. Remove from the oven and let the pumpkin spice breakfast loaf cool in the pan for 10 minutes before transferring it to a wire rack to cool completely.
9. Slice the loaf into 10 slices and serve as a delicious and flavorful breakfast treat.

Nutritional Value (per slice):

Calories: 260 kcal

Protein: 5g

Carbohydrates: 39g

Fiber: 4g

Fat: 10g

Saturated Fat. 1g

Creative Diabetic Breakfast Ideas for Special Occasions

Smoked Salmon and Cream Cheese Bagels (Whole Wheat)

Prep Time: 10 minutes

Cooking Time: 0 minutes

Serve: 2 bagels

Ingredients:

- 2 whole wheat bagels, sliced and toasted
- 4 tablespoons cream cheese (low-fat or regular)
- 4 oz (113g) smoked salmon
- 1/4 red onion, thinly sliced
- 1 tablespoon capers
- Fresh dill sprigs for garnish

Preparation Method:

1. Slice the whole wheat bagels in half and toast them until lightly browned.
2. Spread 2 tablespoons of cream cheese on the bottom half of each bagel.
3. Top the cream cheese with smoked salmon slices.

4. Add a few slices of red onion on top of the smoked salmon.
5. Sprinkle capers over the onions.
6. Garnish with fresh dill sprigs.
7. Top each sandwich with the top half of the bagels.
8. Serve the smoked salmon and cream cheese bagels as a classic and satisfying breakfast option.

Nutritional Value (per bagel sandwich):

Calories: 350 kcal

Protein: 19g

Carbohydrates: 46g

Fiber: 6g

Fat: 10g

Saturated Fat: 4g

Breakfast Quinoa with Roasted Vegetables

Prep Time: 15 minutes

Cooking Time: 25 minutes

Serve: 4

Ingredients:

- 1 cup quinoa, rinsed
- 2 cups vegetable broth or water

- 1 medium sweet potato, peeled and diced
- 1 medium zucchini, diced
- 1 red bell pepper, diced
- 1 tablespoon olive oil
- 1 teaspoon dried thyme
- Salt and pepper to taste
- 4 large eggs
- Fresh parsley for garnish

Preparation Method:

1. Preheat the oven to 425°F (220°C).
2. In a saucepan, bring the vegetable broth or water to a boil.
3. Add the rinsed quinoa to the boiling liquid, reduce the heat to low, cover the saucepan, and let the quinoa simmer for about 15 minutes or until all the liquid is absorbed and the quinoa is fluffy.
4. While the quinoa is cooking, spread the diced sweet potato, diced zucchini, and diced red bell pepper on a baking sheet.
5. Drizzle olive oil over the vegetables and sprinkle dried thyme, salt, and pepper.

6. Toss the veggies in the oil and spice to coat evenly.
7. Roast the veggies for about 20-25 minutes, or until soft and gently browned, tossing once or twice throughout cooking.
8. Fry the eggs to your chosen level of doneness in a separate pan.
9. Divide the cooked quinoa among serving dishes to serve.
10. Add a piece of the roasted veggies to each bowl.
11. Top each dish with a cooked egg.
12. Garnish with fresh parsley.
13. Serve the breakfast quinoa with roasted vegetables for a hearty and nutritious morning meal.

Nutritional Value (per serving):

Calories: 380 kcal

Protein: 15g

Carbohydrates: 51g

Fiber: 8g

Fat: 14g

Saturated Fat: 3g

Stuffed Bell Peppers with Egg and Spinach

Prep Time: 15 minutes

Cooking Time: 25 minutes

Serve: 4 stuffed peppers

Ingredients:

- 4 large bell peppers of any color, halved and removed the seeds
- 1 cup fresh spinach leaves
- 1/2 cup diced tomatoes
- 1/4 cup diced red onion
- 4 large eggs
- 1/2 cup shredded mozzarella cheese (or any preferred cheese)
- 2 tablespoons olive oil
- 1 teaspoon dried oregano
- Salt and pepper to taste
- Fresh basil leaves for garnish

Preparation Method:

1. Preheat the oven to 375°F (190°C). Using parchment paper, line a baking sheet.
2. Warm the olive oil in a pan over medium heat.

3. Sauté the chopped red onion in the pan until it gets transparent.
4. Cook until the spinach wilts, then add the diced tomatoes and fresh spinach leaves.
5. Season the spinach mixture with salt, pepper, and dry oregano.
6. Place the halved bell peppers on the baking sheet that has been prepared.
7. Divide the spinach mixture evenly between the pepper halves.
8. Create a small well in the center of each pepper half to hold the egg.
9. Crack an egg into each well.
10. Sprinkle shredded mozzarella cheese over each egg.
11. Bake in the preheated oven for about 20-25 minutes or until the eggs are cooked to your preferred level of doneness and the peppers are tender.
12. Remove from the oven and let the stuffed bell peppers cool slightly.
13. Garnish with fresh basil leaves.

14. Serve the stuffed bell peppers with egg and spinach for a colorful and nutritious breakfast.

Nutritional Value (per stuffed pepper half):

Calories: 180 kcal

Protein: 8g

Carbohydrates: 9g

Fiber: 2g

Fat: 13g

Saturated Fat: 4g

Vegetable and Feta Frittata Cups

Prep Time: 15 minutes

Cooking Time: 25 minutes

Serve: 6 frittata cups

Ingredients:

6 large eggs

- 1/4 cup milk (any preferred milk)
- 1/2 cup diced bell peppers (any color)
- 1/4 cup diced zucchini
- 1/4 cup diced cherry tomatoes
- 1/4 cup crumbled feta cheese

- 1 tablespoon chopped fresh basil
- 1 tablespoon olive oil
- Salt and pepper to taste

Preparation Method:
1. Preheat the oven to 375°F (190°C). Line a muffin tray with paper liners or grease it.
2. Whisk together the eggs and milk in a large mixing basin until thoroughly blended.
3. Stir in the diced bell peppers, diced zucchini, diced cherry tomatoes, crumbled feta cheese, chopped fresh basil, olive oil, salt, and pepper.
4. Divide the frittata mixture among the muffin cups in the prepared muffin tin.
5. Bake in the preheated oven for about 20-25 minutes or until the frittata cups are set and lightly browned on top.
6. Remove from the oven and let the frittata cups cool slightly before removing them from the muffin tin.
7. Serve the vegetable and feta frittata cups as a flavorful and protein-rich breakfast.

Nutritional Value (per frittata cup):

Calories: 140 kcal

Protein: 8g

Carbohydrates: 3g

Fiber: 1g

Fat: 10g

Saturated Fat: 3g

Sodium: 240mg

Beverages to Complement Diabetic Breakfasts

Sugar-Free Hot Cocoa

Prep Time: 5 minutes

Cooking Time: 5 minutes

Serve: 2 cups

Ingredients:

- 2 cups unsweetened almond milk (or any milk of choice)
- 2 tablespoons unsweetened cocoa powder
- 1/2 teaspoon vanilla extract
- Pinch of salt
- Sugar substitute (stevia, erythritol, or any preferred sweetener) to taste
- Optional toppings: Whipped cream (sugar-free), a sprinkle of cocoa powder

Preparation Method:

1. In a saucepan, heat the unsweetened almond milk over medium heat until it begins to steam. Do not boil

2. Whisk in the unsweetened cocoa powder, vanilla extract, and a pinch of salt until the cocoa powder is fully dissolved.
3. Sweeten the hot cocoa to taste with your preferred sugar substitute, adding it gradually until you reach the desired level of sweetness.
4. Pour the sugar-free hot cocoa into mugs.
5. Optionally, top each mug with a dollop of sugar-free whipped cream and a sprinkle of cocoa powder.
6. Serve the sugar-free hot cocoa as a comforting and guilt-free treat on chilly mornings or any time you crave a cozy beverage.

Nutritional Value (per cup):

Calories: 30 kcal

Protein: 1g

Carbohydrates: 2g

Fiber: 1g

Fat: 2g

Saturated Fat: 0g

Iced Green Tea with Lemon

Prep Time: 5 minutes

Cooking Time: 5 minutes (plus cooling time)

Serve: 2 glasses

Ingredients:

- 2 cups water
- 2 green tea bags
- 1 tablespoon honey
- 1 lemon, sliced
- Ice cubes
- Fresh mint leaves for garnish

Preparation Method:

1. In a saucepan, bring 2 cups of water to a boil.
2. To the boiling water, add the green tea bags or loose green tea leaves.
3. Allow the green tea to steep for 3-5 minutes, depending on your tea strength desire.
4. Remove the tea bags or loose tea leaves and set aside.
5. While the tea is still warm, whisk in the honey or sweetener of choice to dissolve it.

6. Allow the green tea to reach room temperature.
7. Refrigerate the tea for at least 1 hour once it has cooled.
8. Fill two glasses halfway with ice cubes and a couple lemon wedges each.
9. Pour the iced green tea over the lemon slices and ice.
10. Garnish with fresh mint leaves for extra flavor.
11. Serve the iced green tea with lemon as a refreshing and hydrating beverage, perfect for warm mornings or afternoons.

Nutritional Value (per glass):

Calories: 10 kcal

Protein: 0g

Carbohydrates: 3g

Fiber: 0g

Fat: 0g

Saturated Fat: 0g

Sodium: 0mg

Cucumber and Mint Infused Water

Prep Time: 5 minutes

Serve: 2 glasses

Ingredients:

- 4 cups water
- 1/2 cucumber, sliced
- 1/4 cup fresh mint leaves
- Ice cubes

Preparation Method:

1. Combine the sliced cucumber and fresh mint leaves in a pitcher.
2. Pour 4 cups of water into the pitcher.
3. Gently stir to unleash the cucumber and mint tastes.
4. Allow at least 1 hour for the flavors to combine in the infused water.
5. Fill two glasses with ice cubes.
6. Pour the chilled cucumber and mint infused water into the glasses, straining out the cucumber slices and mint leaves.
7. Optionally, garnish with a fresh mint sprig.

8. Serve the cucumber and mint infused water as a refreshing and hydrating option to keep you cool and hydrated throughout the day.

Nutritional Value (per glass):

Calories: 0 kcal

Protein: 0g

Carbohydrates: 0g

Fiber: 0g

Fat: 0g

Infused water, like cucumber and mint infused water, is a hydrating and refreshing beverage that contains very few calories and nutrients since it primarily consists of water with the added flavor of the infused ingredients. The nutritional value of cucumber and mint infused water is minimal, but it offers a great alternative to plain water and can help you stay hydrated.

Low-carb Strawberry Smoothie

Prep Time: 5 minutes

Serve: 2 cups

Ingredients:

- 1 cup unsweetened almond milk (or any milk of choice)
- 1 cup frozen strawberries
- 1/2 cup plain Greek yogurt
- 1 tablespoon almond butter (or any nut butter)
- 1 teaspoon chia seeds
- 1/2 teaspoon vanilla extract
- Sugar substitute (stevia, erythritol, or any preferred sweetener) to taste (optional)
- Ice cubes (optional)

Preparation Method:

1. In a blender, combine the unsweetened almond milk, frozen strawberries, plain Greek yogurt, almond butter, chia seeds, and vanilla extract.
2. Blend until smooth and creamy, adjusting the consistency with ice cubes if desired.
3. Sweeten the smoothie to taste with your preferred sugar substitute, adding it gradually until you reach the desired level of sweetness.

4. Pour the low-carb strawberry smoothie into glasses.
5. Optionally, garnish with a strawberry slice or a sprinkle of chia seeds.
6. Serve the low-carb strawberry smoothie as a delicious and satisfying breakfast or snack option, especially suitable for those following a low-carb lifestyle.

Nutritional Value (per cup):

Calories: 120 kcal

Protein: 6g

Carbohydrates: 10g

Fiber: 3g

Fat: 7g

Saturated Fat: 1g

Conclusion

This collection of diabetic-friendly breakfast recipes provides seniors with a diverse array of nutritious, delicious, and easy-to-prepare options to kick start their day and support their overall health. Understanding the importance of managing diabetes in seniors, these recipes focus on using wholesome, low-carb, and nutrient-dense ingredients while still offering a wide range of flavors and textures to satisfy different tastes.

From quick and simple options like scrambled tofu with veggies and overnight chia seed pudding to more elaborate dishes like spinach and feta egg bake and low-carb strawberry smoothie, these recipes cater to a variety of preferences and dietary needs. Each recipe comes with clear prep and cooking times, essential ingredients, preparation methods, and valuable nutritional information to help seniors make informed choices about their breakfast selections.

Moreover, the inclusion of delightful beverage options like sugar-free hot cocoa, cucumber and mint infused water, and iced green tea with lemon ensures that seniors have hydrating and enjoyable alternatives to complement their meals.

By including these diabetic-friendly breakfast recipes into their daily routine, seniors can fuel their bodies with nourishing ingredients, maintain stable blood sugar levels, and take steps toward achieving a healthier and more balanced lifestyle. Empowered with this compilation of recipes, seniors can embrace their mornings with excitement and confidence, knowing that each meal not only supports their well-being but also brings a burst of flavor and satisfaction to their day.

It is always essential for seniors with diabetes to work closely with their healthcare professionals and dietitians to tailor these recipes to their specific dietary needs and medical conditions. By combining delicious flavors with nutritional benefits, this compilation seeks to provide seniors with a delightful and empowering breakfast experience that contributes to their overall health and happiness.

Printed in Great Britain
by Amazon